PERFECT SEASON • COMMEMORATIVE BOOK

Believe It!

Rose Bowl Win Caps TCU's Perfect Season

UL MOSELEY, STAR-TELEGRAM

Star-Telegram

HORNED FROGS
TCU

TCU players celebrate at midfield to chant "T-C-U Frogs!" after TCU's 21-19 victory in the Rose Bowl.
Paul Moseley, Star-Telegram

This book is available in quantity at special discounts for your group or organization.
For further information contact:

Triumph Books
542 South Dearborn Street
Suite 750
Chicago, IL 60605
Phone: (312) 939-3330
Fax: (312) 663-3557
www.triumphbooks.com

Printed in the United States of America
ISBN: 978-1-60078-609-9

Star-Telegram
Publisher: Gary Wortel
Senior Vice President and Executive Editor: Jim Witt
Vice President Online and Deputy Executive Editor: Ellen Alfano
Managing Editor: Celeste Williams
Sports Editor: Joe Garza
Staff Columnist: Gil LeBreton
Staff writers: Stefan Stevenson and Ray Buck
Staff photographers: Max Faulkner, Ron Jenkins, Joyce Marshall, Ian McVea and Paul Moseley

Content packaged by Mojo Media, Inc.
Joe Funk: Editor
Jason Hinman: Creative Director

Front and back cover photos by Paul Moseley, Star-Telegram.

All photographs by Star-Telegram unless otherwise noted.

Bart Johnson's first-quarter touchdown started TCU on the way to its historic Rose Bowl victory. *Paul Moseley, Star-Telegram*

contents

Foreword

By Gil LeBreton

In the gnawing void of their disappointment, coach Gary Patterson had challenged them. The 2009 TCU Horned Frogs had just been humbled 17-10 on the Fiesta Bowl's prominently lit stage by a team they felt they were superior to, the Boise State Broncos.

And now, in the silence of the locker room, came Patterson's grim assessment.

"I told them, 'You've got to decide,'" he recalled. "'You've got to decide how you want to handle this.'

"It was like when you're growing up, and a kid knocks you down, how are you going to handle it? Are you going to get back up crying, or are you going to get back up, dust yourself off, and move forward from there?"

Moving forward. Forever climbing. As the pyramid chart on the wall of their team meeting room suggests, the Frogs have been taught that if they aren't climbing their way to the top of the college football world, they're standing still.

The penultimate step in Patterson's pyramid of goals reads simply, "Go to BCS game — and win."

"We thought about that line all throughout the off-season," senior quarterback Andy Dalton said. "To us, there was unfinished business."

TCU's history in postseason bowl games is a long and distinguished one, even though some pages of it have long since started to fade at the edges. The Horned Frogs of 1935 played in the second-ever Sugar Bowl. The 1936 Frogs played in the very first Cotton Bowl. Coach Dutch Meyer's 1941 TCU team ended its season in the Orange Bowl.

One glittering jewel was missing.

A first-time clause in the Bowl Championship Series selection guidelines had cracked the door to the Rose Bowl this season for a team from a non-automatically qualifying conference. While the undefeated Frogs, therefore, had one eye—and one Cinderella glass slipper—focused on the race for a spot in the national title game, the season quickly evolved into a contest with Boise State to see which could claim the rare opportunity of a trip to the Rose Bowl.

The Broncos poured it on over weak Western Athletic Conference opposition, averaging 46.7 points a game.

Coach Gary Patterson hoists the Rose Bowl trophy with Rose Bowl Defensive MVP Tank Carder looking on.
Paul Moseley, Star-Telegram

TCU
HORNED FROGS
43

Patterson's answering salvo, meanwhile, was—and likely will always be—his No. 1-ranked defense. TCU held seven of its 12 opponents this season to single digits in scoring.

From Sept. 24 to Nov. 13, a span of nearly two months, the Frogs allowed only three touchdowns.

Three members of the TCU defense—linebacker Tank Carder, defensive end Wayne Daniels and safety Tejay Johnson—were named to All-America teams. Eight Frog defenders made either the first or second All-Mountain West Conference teams.

Patterson's team never stopped climbing. Facing the heart of its MWC schedule, the Frogs knocked off BYU, Air Force and Utah by a combined score of 116-17.

The BCS giveth, the BCS taketh away.

We'll never know how the victorious Frogs would have done in the title game. But a triumph over a pedigreed Big Ten foe, Wisconsin 21-19, merits a ringing validation.

To many TCU fans, reared on the three-alarm chili of the defunct Southwest Conference, the Rose Bowl has always been a New Year's Day interlude. A game played by storied, but distant, football programs amidst a mountain-fringed backdrop that looked like a Hollywood movie set.

But a rose is a rose is a rose.

On Monday before the big game, Patterson took his team to Pasadena to see the famous old stadium for the first time. The Frogs' reverence quickly became apparent.

They posed for pictures. Some leaned over, brushing their hands across the immaculately trimmed turf. Their necks craned to take in the dramatic backdrop of the San Gabriel Mountains.

At the north end, a group of Frogs players gathered to watch the end zone being painted a rich purple with the letters "TCU" prominently in the center.

For TCU, a team that had been abandoned on the doorstep when the SWC folded, it was a powerful moment.

From the tragedy of coach Jim Pittman's death on the sideline in 1971, to the collapse of the program later in the '70s and the bitter NCAA sanctions handed to it in 1986, the climb back has been a monumental one.

If the Frogs didn't at first grasp the uniqueness of the bowl game that's called The Granddaddy of Them All, they quickly learned.

Late in the season, the bow-tied president of Ohio State, Dr. E. Gordon Gee, had taken a misguided swipe at TCU and Boise by chiding them for not playing the "murderer's row" schedule that Big Ten teams do. For the Frogs, therefore, the timeliness of their historic first victory in the Rose Bowl could not have been more appropriate.

The final tip in Patterson's pyramid—a national championship—remains. But that's a climb for another season.

For this time, this undefeated TCU team, a Rose was a Rose was a Rose.

The memories will be forever. ■

Cornerback Greg McCoy breaks up a pass intended for Wisconsin receiver Nick Toon during the second half. Wisconsin quarterback Scott Tolzien completed only 12 of 21 passes against the nation's top defense. *Paul Moseley, Star-Telegram*

TCU
McCOY
7
TCU

TCU 21, Wisconsin 19
January 1, 2011 • Pasadena, California

TCU finishes perfect season with Rose Bowl win

By Stefan Stevenson

Defense has been TCU's calling card since the football program began its rise in the late 1990s under coach Gary Patterson.

So it was only fitting that the defense rose to the challenge Saturday with a game-saving play in the final minutes of the 97th Rose Bowl in front of a crowd of 94,118.

With two minutes remaining, Frogs linebacker Tank Carder knocked down Wisconsin quarterback Scott Tolzien's pass on a 2-point conversion attempt to preserve the historic 21-19 victory.

Third-ranked TCU finished 13-0, recording the school's first perfect season since the national title year of 1938 and the most wins in a season in school history.

"On the last play, I figured it was going to be a run," said Carder, who was named Rose Bowl defensive MVP after recording six tackles, including a sack and two others for losses. "I went to go blitz and got blocked and couldn't get through the hole. So I stopped, backed up, saw him cock his arm back, and I jumped."

The pass breakup gave the Frogs offense–which was outgained 385 to 301 yards–a chance to run out the final two minutes.

Waymon James' two runs for 6 and 5 yards got the first down, and Andy Dalton, who has led the TCU offense the last four seasons, took a knee on the last two plays before being mobbed by teammates as confetti shot into the air.

TCU, playing in its first Rose Bowl and second consecutive Bowl Championship Series game, defeated Big Ten power Wisconsin (11-2), despite losing the first-down battle (20-18) and trailing in time of possession by 13 minutes.

"We only got the ball three times in the first half," said Dalton, who led the Frogs' senior class to a school-record 44 wins. "We knew we had to take advantage of our opportunities because Wisconsin has such a good run offense."

Andy Dalton completed 15 of 23 passes for one touchdown and ran for another score. *Paul Moseley, Star-Telegram*

TCU
14
HORNED FROGS
14

Bart Johnson celebrates after his 23-yard touchdown puts TCU up 7–3 in the first quarter of the Rose Bowl. *Paul Moseley, Star-Telegram*

Dalton's final performance was one of the best of his storied career. He threw for 219 yards and accounted for two touchdowns in the first half: a 23-yard pass to Bart Johnson and a 4-yard run to the corner of the end zone to give TCU the lead for good at 14-10 in the final seconds of the first quarter. Dalton completed 15 of 23 passes and was barely touched in the backfield.

"We took a lot of offense," TCU senior center Jake Kirkpatrick said of the media's fawning over the Badgers' big offensive line throughout the week. "Wisconsin has a good line, but no one said a word about us. We took pride in it tonight and tried to give Andy some time. We're Rose Bowl champions because of Andy. I wouldn't want to play for anyone else."

Although fourth-ranked Wisconsin moved the ball, the Frogs defense was able to hold the Badgers to field goals twice, including the game's opening possession. Montee Ball sprang loose for 40 yards on Wisconsin's first play from scrimmage, but a defensive stand by the Frogs held the Badgers to a 30-yard field goal.

TCU immediately answered with a 10-play, 77-yard drive that ended with Dalton's strike to Johnson. Wisconsin swiftly reclaimed the lead with John Clay's 1-yard run that capped a six-play, 67-yard drive. Tolzien connected on three passes of 14 yards or more on the drive, including a 28-yarder to Bradie Ewing to TCU's 1.

"These guys are really good at what they do," TCU defensive end Wayne Daniels said of the Badgers. "After that, I figured that was their best shot. We settled down a little bit and started playing the way we know how to play."

Tank Carder takes down Wisconsin quarterback Scott Tolzien in the third quarter. Wisconsin was forced to punt on the next play.
Paul Moseley, Star-Telegram

MOFFITT
74

Jeremy Kerley's 35-yard return on the ensuing kickoff ignited the Frogs' second drive. Dalton, who led TCU in rushing with 28 yards, found Josh Boyce open downfield for a 44-yard gain. Dalton then ran three consecutive times, the last a 4-yard scamper to the left pylon.

"What better way to go out than with a Rose Bowl victory?" asked Kerley, a senior. "Dalton is a stallion quarterback. I knew that since the first day I stepped on campus. I'm glad he performed today."

Dalton connected with Ed Wesley for 33 yards and Jimmy Young for 12 yards on the Frogs' first drive of the second half. After Matthew Tucker's 12-yard run put the ball on the 1, Luke Shivers plunged into the end zone to give TCU a 21-13 lead.

"To have a game on a stage like this is a perfect accompaniment for me and the team," said Young, who had five receptions for 57 yards.

"We just took what they gave us. The coaches did a good job of seeing what they were giving us, and we did a good job of executing and taking advantage of it. It's the perfect way to go out."

Patterson, who has often talked about TCU "climbing the mountain" with a national title, will, for now, settle for a perfect season.

"Right now, 13-0 is top of the mountain," he said.

	1	2	3	4	T
WIS	10	3	0	6	19
TCU	14	0	7	0	21

TCU players celebrate with the Rose Bowl trophy after becoming the first Mountain West team to win the Rose Bowl.
Paul Moseley, Star-Telegram

15
Schutt
Mtn. WEST
TCU
HORNED FROGS

Andy Dalton beats a Wisconsin defender to the end zone for a 4-yard touchdown in the first quarter that put TCU up 14-10. *Paul Moseley, Star-Telegram*

The Frogs are deserving Rose Bowl champions

By Gil LeBreton

In the end, as it rained confetti, they hugged and shouted into the night. And, truth be known, there were tears of joy in some of the eyes that now peered out from under their new caps.

The caps, like the new T-shirts, that proclaimed, "TCU 2011 Rose Bowl Champions."

For the TCU Horned Frogs, a rose will never quite be just a rose ever again.

On the eve of this 97th Rose Bowl game, TCU coach Gary Patterson had been asked at a news conference how the nation would perceive a victory by the Frogs over a pedigreed Big Ten team such as Wisconsin.

Patterson, though, had turned the question around.

"If we do win, how are you going to write it?" Patterson said, challenging the audience. "Are you going to write that it's because Wisconsin didn't play well? Or are you going to write that we played a great ballgame?"

After Saturday's hard-earned 21-19 victory over the Wisconsin Badgers, Patterson need not be worried.

For 60 minutes, the Badgers pounded away at the belly of the TCU defense. For 60 minutes, on both sides, there were no interceptions, no lost fumbles and few penalties.

In its 96 previous renditions, there might have been better Rose Bowls. But there can't be many.

Not many so rich in parable and redemption. Not many where one of the competing teams had come so far—literally and figuratively.

And not many Rose Bowls where the winning team had cried real and happy tears.

"I don't know if I can describe it," said tight ends coach Dan Sharp, who played on TCU teams (1981-84) that won a total of only 14 games.

"It took so long, and we've come so far. And we're here. It's unbelievable."

History will record that this TCU-Wisconsin Rose Bowl was decided on a timely deflection. Wisconsin coach Bret Bielema is certain to be criticized for his decision to call a pass play on the

Wide receiver Josh Boyce hauls in a 44-yard pass from Andy Dalton in the first quarter. The play set up Dalton's 4-yard touchdown run three plays later. *Paul Moseley, Star-Telegram*

BigTen
Riddell
VIZIO
82
adidas
TCU

Andy Dalton hands off to running back Waymon Jame
during the first quarter. James gained 24 yards on fou
carries for the Frogs. *Paul Moseley, Star-Telegram*

schutt
TCU
FROGS
NIKE
14
32
VIZIO
NIKE PRO
TCU
TCU

Badgers' 2-point conversion try rather than putting the game's fate in the hands of the powerful, well-rested and seemingly unstoppable John Clay.

"They had the right play called," Patterson suggested, "because we had a run blitz called.

"Sometimes, though, you just have to make a play."

Sometimes, even in the Rose Bowl, Goliath doesn't go down with just one rock. Sensing a quick slant on the 2-point play, TCU linebacker Tank Carder reacted instinctively to quarterback Scott Tolzien's pass and spanked the ball away.

The purple-clad fans roared. Carder walked to the TCU sideline, and a congratulatory swarm of teammates engulfed him.

The TCU offense ran out the final two minutes.

Somehow, despite giving up 226 yards rushing, TCU's nation-leading defense rose to make the game-deciding play.

Unlike a year ago, when TCU mistakes scuttled the Frogs' first BCS bowl encounter, Patterson's team played a turnover-free game. The Frogs held to 19 points a Big Ten offense that had scored 83 points on Indiana and 70 on Northwestern.

"Do you have any sense of how well you played?" a postgame questioner asked.

"No," Patterson answered, "because it seemed like they rushed for about 1,500 yards and threw for over 2,000."

Actually, Wisconsin's total yardage was 385. There were plays—great plays, as it turned out—left in the Rose Bowl Frogs.

"Look at this," Patterson said sheepishly, after

Tank Carder, left, reacts with teammates after sacking Wisconsin quarterback Scott Tolzien in the third quarter. Carder knocked down a potential 2-point conversion pass with minutes left in the game to seal the victory.
Paul Moseley, Star-Telegram

TCU
90
ORNED FROGS
90
FROGS
TCU

the game in a nearly-empty TCU locker room. He held out his cellphone.

"175 text messages," the phone read. "Network authenticity failed."

The Frogs had been unable to stop Clay on that final drive. But they ended up bringing an entire phone network to its knees.

So how will it be written, this latest chapter in the TCU football fairy tale? Will people dwell on what the Big Ten Badgers didn't do, or will it finally be the affirmation that the Frogs truly belong?

"I'll say this," Patterson said. "They'll never be able to take it away from us.

"People can say what they want, but it'll be our name up on that wall—Rose Bowl champions."

Fifteen years ago, the TCU football program was left orphaned and alone on the defunct Southwest Conference's doorstep. On Saturday, the Frogs won the Rose Bowl in one of college football's most hallowed settings, in front of a live audience of 94,118.

"I actually caught myself thinking that," Patterson confessed.

"I thought, 'Well, we get back tomorrow, but nobody will there to meet us, I guess, because they're all here.'"

He laughed. He was happy. He had a cap on his locker room desk that read, "TCU 2011 Rose Bowl Champions."

And one of college football's greatest comeback stories had written a unique and glorious chapter.

That's how I'm writing it, at least.

The tears are optional.

Center Jake Kirkpatrick marches toward the stands with the Rose Bowl trophy held high. *Paul Moseley, Star-Telegram*

TCU
HORNED FROGS
76
HORNED FROGS
64
15
4

TCU

The TCU Horned Frog Band marches with the team's Rose Bowl float during the annual New Year's Day Rose Parade. *Paul Moseley, Star-Telegram*

Gary Patterson

TCU coach takes to the national airwaves to make case for Frogs

By Ray Buck

Gary Patterson easily picked up the media blitz on Friday, Nov. 19. The coach of the BCS No. 3-ranked TCU Horned Frogs accepted an all-day invitation to ESPN headquarters in Bristol, Conn., and effectively turned it into a series of soapbox opportunities.

He appeared on multiple ESPN media platforms. His one basic message: We belong with the big boys.

Patterson appeared both relaxed and well-prepared for his "Car Wash" treatment, as the network calls it, starting out with Mike & Mike in the Morning for the 8:15 a.m. segment.

Patterson, whose Frogs were idle that weekend, grabbed lunch in the ESPN cafeteria, appeared on a few more shows, then hopped a jet to Chicago, where he made a 9:20 a.m. appearance Saturday, Nov. 20, on the set of ESPN College GameDay from Wrigley Field.

Here are a few highlights from Gary's busy Friday:

8:18 a.m.—Patterson appears on camera behind a sea of bobbleheads on the Mike & Mike set. An oversized microphone (it's a radio show simulcast on TV) obscures his jaw and most of his mouth... but he's attired in a black jacket worn over a black TCU golf shirt, obviously from the Johnny Cash Collection. And, no, he's not wearing a visor.

8:19 a.m.—Co-host Mike Greenberg introduces him as "a man I am rooting for like crazy," adding that either Boise State or TCU—both undefeated—deserves a chance to play for the national championship if one of the higher-ranked undefeated teams—Oregon or Auburn—pick up a loss.

8:21 a.m.—"I get a little bit tired that the only comparison that people want to make is [between] Boise and TCU," Patterson says. "I feel like there are four unbeaten teams in college football, and one of the reasons we came on ESPN today is to say that we feel like we belong."

8:24 a.m.—Patterson gets on a roll. "I love college football, not only as a coach but also as a fan. The problem I have is that I think we should watch this closely and not lose the fans... [and] make sure we do things for the right reason."

8:25 a.m.—Patterson tells the two Mikes: "Thanks for sticking up for us."

Head coach Gary Patterson raises his fist in celebration during the fourth quarter of TCU's Sept. 24 win over SMU. TCU's fourth win of 2010 was its 10th in its past 11 games against rival SMU. *Ron Jenkins, Star-Telegram*

TCU
21
TCU

10:23 a.m.—On First Take with Mike Hill, Patterson is seated in a cushy armchair. The shot includes a table arrangement of a TCU helmet and a football.

10:25 a.m.—For the second time, he brings up his deep belief in "the American way"—i.e., a chance to prove yourself—and college football being committed to getting it right. That's also the American way, he is quick to add.

10:45 a.m.—Patterson's scheduled appearance on The Herd with Colin Cowherd is scratched. Cowherd, instead of doing the Friday show from Bristol, is live from Dan Marino's restaurant in Miami.

11:30 a.m.—Mark Cohen, TCU media relations director, is on his cellphone from the ESPN cafeteria. "A warm welcome for the Frogs. They love us, it seems. It's fantastic exposure," Cohen reports. "You run into so many [TV personalities] you know. It's an all-lobby team just hanging out in the green room."

1:36 p.m.—On radio, Patterson gets seven minutes on the Scott Van Pelt Show. "I've never been one to discount any [team] out there," Gary says. "I'm just very proud of my football team. That's why I'm here today... to let people know what kind of people and what kind of football team we have at TCU."

2:17 p.m.—He moves back to TV—SportsCenter, no less—and sits on a high director's chair opposite Cindy Brunson. There's a scratchy sound problem. Patterson talks about climbing the mountain as a football program. Segment lasts four minutes.

2:36 p.m.—As a guest on College Football Live, Patterson seems much more comfortable in an overstuffed chair. It's a 30-minute show. He's on-camera for 12.

2:40 p.m.—Patterson has stopped voting in the coaches poll, but says he'd put TCU in the top 3, then later revises it to No. 1, explaining with a wry smile, "You have to be biased." Everyone else is.

2:58 p.m.—Patterson wishes every team good luck, then adds, "I'm here [because] I owe it to my team" to let the world know that the Horned Frogs are worthy of playing on the biggest stage in college football. ■

Gary Patterson smiles during practice in Carson, Calif., on Dec. 28 before facing Wisconsin in the Rose Bowl on New Year's Day.
AP Images

TCU
TCU

Quarterback Andy Dalton and coach Gary Patterson celebrate following TCU's Sept. 24 win over SMU. After falling behind 17-14 in the third quarter, the Frogs scored touchdowns on three straight drives and won 41-24. *Ron Jenkins, Star-Telegram*

TCU
TCU

TCU 30, Oregon State 21
September 4, 2010 • Arlington, Texas

Thank you, Lee Corso

By Stefan Stevenson

Gary Patterson is always looking for motivational tools. Saturday morning he didn't have to look far.

ESPN College GameDay's Lee Corso predicted TCU would lose by three touchdowns to Oregon State. Patterson was watching and made sure his team knew about it before their season opener against the Beavers at Cowboys Stadium.

The sixth-ranked Horned Frogs took the motivational tool and put to rest any doubts about their chances of making a second consecutive BCS bowl run with a 30-21 win in front of 46,138 in attendance.

It was the Frogs' eighth consecutive victory to open a season.

But it was anything but easy.

The Frogs (1-0) rushed for 278 yards, including Ed Wesley's 134 yards on 17 carries. Matthew Tucker added 74 yards, while quarterback Andy Dalton rushed for 64 yards and two touchdowns, the last one coming on a 4-yard run to cap a 71-yard drive that gave TCU a 28-21 lead at the end of the third quarter.

No. 24 Oregon State (0-1), which had taken advantage of two interceptions earlier in the game, made a costly mistake of its own to ice the win for the Frogs. Beavers quarterback Ryan Katz had a snap sail over his head deep in Oregon State territory and had to kick it out of the back of the end zone for a safety. That gave TCU a 30-21 lead and the ball back with 4:14 remaining.

"The safety was big," Patterson said. "You go up by nine and you play the game a lot different."

TCU's offensive line led a final drive to run out the clock.

Early Saturday night, the game had an awfully familiar feel to the Frogs' last outing, a 17-10 loss in the Fiesta Bowl in January.

Dalton was picked off on the Frogs' first possession and the Oregon State scored two plays later on a 30-yard touchdown pass from Katz to James Rodgers.

Later in the half, the Beavers converted a fake punt for a first down and a play later scored on a 34-yard touchdown pass from Katz to Jordan Bishop to go up 14-7.

"They're a good football team and they're going to win a lot of games," Patterson said of Oregon

TCU safety Colin Jones takes down Oregon State running back Jacquizz Rodgers during the third quarter. The Frogs defense limited Rodgers, the 2008 Pac-10 Offensive Player of the Year, to just 75 net rushing yards. *Max Faulkner, Star-Telegram*

schutt
MAPONGA
90

State. "I think the heat made a difference in the third and fourth quarters."

The stadium roof was opened shortly before kickoff and the outside temperature may have worn down the Beavers in the second half.

The Frogs started to take control of the line of scrimmage in the second quarter and made a decision to work the running game more. It paid off as TCU marched 74 yards in seven running plays to tie the score at 14-14 on a 1-yard touchdown pass from Dalton to Jeremy Kerley.

After Kerley set up the Frogs with great field position on a 33-yard punt return, Wesley, behind the blocks of Jake Kirkpatrick and Zach Roth, scored from 8 yards to put the Frogs back up 21-14 just before the half.

The Frogs' offense was rolling again to start the

(above) Members of the TCU team pour onto the field at Cowboys Stadium prior to the season-opening game against Oregon State. (opposite) Running back Ed Wesley fights for extra yardage as Oregon State's Lance Mitchell tries to bring him down. Wesley gained 134 yards on the ground to lead TCU. *AP Images*

BEAVS
TCU
34
FROGS
35
14

second half, but Dalton threw his second pick deep in Beavers territory. Oregon State drove 87 yards for a 1-yard touchdown run by Jacquizz Rodgers to tie it 21-21.

But the Frogs answered as Dalton led a 12-play, 71-yard drive, which he capped off with a 4-yard run to reclaim the lead 28-21 as the third quarter came to a close.

"I didn't let those interceptions affect me," Dalton said. "I knew I had to come back and play well to win this game. At times I made some stupid mistakes but felt like I also made a couple [key] plays in the game."

Ground 'n' pound—The Horned Frogs relied on a dominant running game as running backs Ed Wesley and Matthew Tucker and quarterback Andy Dalton totaled 272 yards on the ground.

Steady Dalton—Andy Dalton didn't have his best performance, throwing a pair of interceptions, but he remained poised, and he rushed for seven third-down conversions.

Big winner—Dalton also ran for a pair of touchdowns to record his 30th career victory and pass the legendary Sammy Baugh for the most wins by a TCU quarterback.

Ready to roll?—TCU knocked off one of the biggest threats on its schedule Saturday night. None of the Frogs' remaining opponents is ranked.

	1	2	3	4	T
OSU	7	7	7	0	21
TCU	7	14	7	2	30

Offensive guards Josh Vernon (78) and Blaize Foltz (66) and teammates celebrate with the Cowboys Stadium crowd after defeating Oregon State in the season-opening Cowboys Classic. *Max Faulkner, Star-Telegram*

at&t
Ford
Mtn. WEST
TCU
HORNED FROGS
66
HORNED FROGS
78
61

TCU 62, Tennessee Tech 7
September 11, 2010 • Fort Worth, Texas

As expected, the No. 4-ranked Horned Frogs had little trouble

By Stefan Stevenson

When your team rolls to a dominating 62-7 victory, you'd think there'd be little to complain about.

But not for TCU coach Gary Patterson. He wasn't celebrating Saturday night

In fact, he was packing up his laptop, taking a shower and planning on watching tape of next Saturday's opponent: 2-0 Baylor.

He wasn't in any mood to relish the win over Football Championship Subdivision team Tennessee Tech (0-2). He was too distracted by a sloppy stretch of play by the Frogs after they had taken a 21-point first-quarter lead.

But before Patterson could even get to that during his postgame news conference, he apologized to Tennessee Tech for scoring the final touchdown with 4:09 left in the fourth quarter.

"I want to publicly apologize," Patterson said. "I didn't mean to score the last touchdown. We don't do style points. We didn't throw the ball in the fourth quarter. That's not the program we are, period. I did not want to score 60. I don't think [Tennessee Tech coach Watson Brown] is very happy with me."

But TCU wasn't trying to run up the score. On the play in question, fifth-year senior Ryan Hightower, who was playing in just his fourth career game, cut around the left side on a run and had nothing in front of him but an open 16-yard path to the end zone.

"I'm not going to come in here and jump up and down," Patterson said. "I was really excited for Ryan Hightower. We were just running a fullback for a couple of yards, but he cut back. It was not called to get a touchdown. I'm happy for him. He's been doing it for five years and never gets any credit. But I've been on the other end of it, and I just don't like those kinds of games."

The fourth-ranked Frogs (2-0) dominated from the beginning, scoring on a 24-yard pass from Andy Dalton to Josh Boyce on their first possession. TCU took a 21-point lead at the end of the

TCU running back Matthew Tucker gains yardage in the second half against Tennessee Tech. The sophomore running back totaled 53 yards on nine carries in the victory. *Joyce Marshall, Star-Telegram*

TCU
29

first quarter on Jason Teague's 29-yard interception return for a touchdown.

But the Frogs took a nap in the second quarter and blew several opportunities to blow the game wide open with a rash of penalties. Jeremy Kerley had a long kickoff return negated by an illegal block and an incidental facemask on a sack turned a 10-yard sack into a 15-yard first down for Tennessee Tech, which scored its touchdown later on the drive.

"I'm not unhappy," Patterson said. "But we have [issues] we need to make sure we take care of. We played a lot of guys. We didn't get anybody hurt in the game. We went about our business."

TCU took its 15th consecutive victory at Amon G. Carter Stadium and scored its most points since defeating Stephen F. Austin 67-7 in Week 2 in 2008.

"We did have some mistakes," said Dalton, who set a TCU record for most career completions. "But for us to go out and get a win tonight was big. We weren't clean, we weren't fluid on everything we were doing offensively and that's just something we have to fix this week."

TCU, despite the problems, still gained 452 yards of offense (including 270 rushing) and limited the Golden Eagles to 150 total yards.

The Frogs' defense forced six fumbles (recovering four) and held Tech to 55 plays despite the Golden Eagles holding the time of possession edge (31:27 to 28:33).

Matthew Tucker's 1-yard run gave TCU a 35-7 lead at the half. By the fourth quarter Casey Pachall was in the game replacing Dalton and

Senior Alonzo Adams eludes Tennessee Tech defenders on an 11-yard reception in the second quarter.
Joyce Marshall, Star-Telegram

TCU
schutt
HORNED FROGS
81
81
66

Waymon James and Aundre Dean were in for Ed Wesley and Tucker.

"That's what you're supposed to do to a [Division] I-AA team," Patterson said. "But we made too many mistakes. Too many holdings, too many jumps, too many false formations, too many problems."

Kerley, who also had a long punt return negated by a penalty, has been close to taking a kick back two weeks in a row.

"Can't be too mad when you have guys blocking hard for you," said Kerley, who scored two touchdowns on returns last season. "Things will happen like that. We have a high level of play we want to obtain every game and we didn't come out and attack.

"We just have to work on finishing and playing with that lead. People perceive the game [as a great performance], but we know what it was. We have to make up for those mistakes."

By the end of his 10-minute news conference Patterson had moved on to Baylor.

"I'm not enjoying this game at all," he said. "It's time to move forward. Next Saturday we have to stop a very potent offense and we have to be ready to play. [My team] needed to start acting like the fourth-ranked team in the nation. As some point in time they need to take ownership. Bigger ballgames, starting with Baylor this week, you can't make those kinds of mistakes."

	1	2	3	4	T
TTU	0	7	0	0	7
TCU	21	14	6	21	62

Sophomore linebacker Tanner Brock takes down Tennessee Tech wide receiver Tim Benford in the first half. Brock tied for the team lead with nine tackles as the Frogs limited the Golden Eagles to 150 yards. *Brandon Wade, Special to the Star-Telegram*

TCU
28
IBILOY

Andy Dalton

The redhead from Katy is driven to succeed

By Stefan Stevenson

Jeff Ballard was TCU's returning quarterback when he first met Andy Dalton. Ballard had won the last eight games of the 2005 season after taking over for the injured Ty Gunn in Week 5 and was the acknowledged starter for his senior season in 2006.

But Dalton, a somewhat unheralded 18-year-old out of high school powerhouse Katy, joked to Ballard during the spring that he'd start the season opener against Baylor.

"I was sort of thinking, 'Man, this kid is cocky,'" Ballard recalled.

Even if the redheaded youngster was only kidding, it took Ballard aback so much that he remembers commenting at the time, "That's a bold statement to make to the starting quarterback who hadn't lost a game yet.

"But as soon as I thought about it, that's the kind of guy you want to come in and push you and compete with you," said Ballard, who finished 19-2 as the Frogs' starting quarterback. "It wasn't a show of arrogance, it was a show of confidence. He knew he could come in and play at this level."

In truth, Dalton was as nervous about playing as any freshman, even if he was considered TCU's quarterback of the future.

When Ballard was injured in the 2006 season opener against Baylor, sophomore Marcus Jackson was called on to save the day. Jackson started slowly, but led the Frogs to a 17-7 victory in Waco. After a couple of early incompletions by Jackson, Dalton swallowed hard on the sideline.

"Oh, gosh. I was nervous," Dalton remembers. Dalton fretted again later in the season when Jackson had to replace Ballard against Utah.

Dalton never got in a game as a true freshman and was redshirted. When spring rolled around, he was competing with Jackson for the starting spot. It was a battle that lasted into August before Dalton got the nod from former offensive coordinator Mike Schultz. He would be the starter for the 2007 season opener.

"It was a great feeling," Dalton said. "I called my parents and told them the news. I just felt really blessed just to have the opportunity to come in and play right away."

TCU quarterback Andy Dalton was named the Mountain West Conference's Offensive Player of the Year after the 2009 and 2010 seasons. *Richard W. Rodriguez, Special to the Star-Telegram*

Mtn.
WEST
BALANCE

To be playing at all

The fact that Dalton earned the starting job as a redshirt freshman came as no surprise to those who knew him at Katy High School.

But few outside of Katy knew of Dalton because he split time with another quarterback his junior season. Dalton only threw 60 passes that year and wasn't even sure he could play football in college. Luckily, 10 of those passes were for touchdowns, so Greg Dalton, Andy's father, was able to send highlight tapes to colleges.

"I can remember during Andy's junior year being unable to sleep, wondering how he's ever going to play college football," said Greg Dalton, who played quarterback at Houston Memorial in 1977. His son chose No. 14 in honor of his father, who wore 14 in high school.

Andy Dalton wasn't a known quantity in the spring of 2005 when most blue-chip recruits were hearing from all the big-time programs.

That spring, Andy, Greg and Dalton's mother, Tina, made a trip to Fort Worth to visit TCU and watch a practice.

"We actually showed up at the TCU football offices with a tape of Andy," Greg Dalton said. "They had canceled football practice that day, which we were disappointed about."

When TCU coach Gary Patterson walked into the room, Tina said, Patterson didn't know them from anybody, much less that Andy was a quarterback.

"He stopped and spent 30 minutes with us," she said. "We didn't really know about TCU. It was just a nice atmosphere. He's a very busy man, and he spent time with us not knowing who we were. I think we were all impressed that he would take the time."

Dalton, the potential recruit, might have flown under the radar before his senior season, but his five touchdown passes in Week 1 against The Woodlands at Reliant Stadium certainly opened some eyes. Only UT-El Paso and Memphis had offered Dalton a scholarship before his senior season. By October, Dalton was halfway through a 42-touchdown year and the buzz was building when TCU officially made its overture.

After the Frogs' Oct. 15 win over Army, Dalton got a chance to hang out with the TCU quarterbacks, including Gunn, Ballard and Chad Huffman. Dalton asked the group about choosing the right college.

"How do you know when it's right?" he asked.

Huffman responded: "Andy, the Lord is going to tell you. You're going to know because it's going to feel right."

Later, the devout Dalton told his parents, "TCU feels right."

Andy Dalton is swarmed by fans after TCU's come-from-behind victory over San Diego State. Dalton threw for three touchdowns as the Frogs won their last home game before a major off-season renovation of 80-year-old Amon G. Carter Stadium.
Ian McVea, Star-Telegram

SIDELINE

Driven to win

No matter who is describing Dalton—coaches, teammates, parents—his confidence is at the core of his success. He's rewritten nearly every passing record at TCU, including 39 wins as a starting quarterback, surpassing Horned Frogs legend Sammy Baugh earlier this season.

It's that unwavering confidence that has helped Dalton shake off criticisms that all quarterbacks endure. He experienced a taste of it even at Katy.

"I just try not to pay attention to it because everybody has an opinion, and if everything is not going great, everyone's favorite person is the backup quarterback," Dalton said. "That's everywhere."

But for most of his stellar career, Dalton has been the unquestioned starter. In the biggest regular-season game of his career, he threw for a career-high 355 yards and three touchdowns to lead the Frogs past then-No. 6 Utah 47-7. But Dalton was unconcerned with the personal achievement. It was the win that mattered to him.

"It's good to see him play well on a big stage," TCU co-offensive coordinator Justin Fuente said. "A kid like that who works so hard and is so diligent and is such a good person, it always makes you feel good when you see him do it."

Ballard took part in a halftime ceremony Saturday, Nov. 13, along with more than 400 former TCU players, trainers and support staff, to help say goodbye, on Senior Day, to Amon G. Carter Stadium before the 80-year-old venue undergoes a massive renovation. The TCU program has grown by leaps and bounds since Ballard took the snaps years ago, and Dalton's success doesn't surprise him.

"The one thing that does kind of surprise me is he is the third-leading rusher on the team," Ballard said. "Andy Dalton coming out of Katy, Texas, that's the last thing I thought he would be is a runner. He turned into a complete quarterback."

His former quarterbacks coach at Katy, Jeff Rhoads, now the offensive coordinator at Austin Westlake, exchanges texts with Dalton and they talk by phone regularly. Rhoads isn't surprised by Dalton's success, either. It was Dalton's mental makeup, shaped by his parents, Rhoads said, that made it obvious the quarterback would achieve great heights.

"When you have a kid as driven as Andy, it doesn't surprise me," Rhoads said. "The fact he'll be in the NFL next year doesn't surprise me. Every once in a while one comes along that really gets it and has 'it' at the same time. That's Andy.

"I always tell my kids, 'The mind is to the body as 3 is to 1,'" Rhoads continued. "Andy exemplifies that statement more than anybody I've ever seen." ■

Andy Dalton speaks during TCU's Monday night worship meeting, Ignite. Dalton's faith was a major factor in his choice to attend TCU.
Ron Jenkins, Star-Telegram

TCU 45, Baylor 10
September 18, 2010 • Fort Worth, Texas

A 35-3 halftime lead shows how big the gap is

By Stefan Stevenson

Maybe this isn't such a rivalry. TCU's dominating 45-10 victory over Baylor on Saturday was so lopsided that maybe Bears coach Art Briles had it right when he downplayed the tensions between the two schools earlier in the week.

Briles probably knew that as talented as his quarterback is—and Robert Griffin showed flashes of it in front of a sold-out Amon G. Carter Stadium—he wasn't likely to have much time to find his receivers or room to run against TCU's vaunted defense.

And with authority, the Horned Frogs made sure that was the case.

Fourth-ranked TCU (3-0) held Baylor to 263 total yards and kept Griffin scrambling from the outset. Most of those yards (176) were collected in the second half after TCU led 35-3 at halftime. The Bears (2-1) were held to a 48-yard field goal by Crowley's Aaron Jones in the first quarter and didn't score their lone touchdown until Griffin found Josh Gordon deep down the sidelines for a 53-yard touchdown pass late in the third quarter.

"We got down so quick that it became a Catch-22," Briles said. "We didn't really get set with our game plan; we lost it about halfway through the first quarter."

As dominating as the Frogs' defense was, it was the offense that came out and struck early. Andy Dalton completed his first 11 passes and led TCU on touchdown drives on its first five possessions. Dalton finished with a TCU single-game record for completion percentage (91.3 percent), connecting on 21 of 23 passes for 267 yards and two touchdowns.

TCU amassed 558 yards of offense, the most since racking up 578 yards against UNLV last October. Ed Wesley rushed for a career-high 165 yards and two touchdowns, including a 49-yard scoring run to make it 14-0 in the first quarter.

"I wasn't surprised," TCU coach Gary Patterson said of the offense. "We have a senior quarterback and a bunch of guys back. I think you have to give [the offense] a little bit of credit."

Gary Patterson and his team observe the action during TCU's dominating 45-10 win over in-state rival Baylor. The Frogs improved to 3-0. *Ron Jenkins, Star-Telegram*

FROGS
TCU
RNED FROGS
16
27
TCU
TCU

Dalton used 10 receivers effectively, including tight ends Logan Brock and Evan Frosch.

"It was good to get the first [reception] of the season out of the way," said Brock, whose 29-yard reception set up the Frogs' fourth touchdown. "We knew if it was a certain kind of coverage it had to go to me or Evan, and Andy put it on us with good throws."

Dalton moved the offense quickly and systematically. The Frogs had scoring drives of 80, 73, 73 and 90 yards to start the game. These weren't long, laborious drives, either. The longest took 4 minutes, 7 seconds.

(above) TCU's Logan Sligar (59), Spencer Thompson (77) and Trevius Jones (68) sing along with their teammates and the home crowd during the Frogs' 45-10 victory over Baylor. *AP Images*
(opposite) Wide receiver Bart Johnson eludes Baylor defensive end Kevin Park. Johnson's 37-yard fourth quarter reception set up TCU's final touchdown. *Ron Jenkins, Star-Telegram*

BAYLOR

"We were just taking what they were giving us and not trying to do too much," Dalton said. "My job is just to get those guys the ball and they made plays."

Patterson was also happy with the way his team improved on some details from last week's 62-7 victory against Tennessee Tech. TCU played turnover-free and had only three penalties for 25 yards. The Frogs were penalized seven times against Tennessee Tech, despite dominating the game. Once again both TCU lines dictated the game. TCU sacked Griffin three times and had him bailing out of the pocket on nearly every pass attempt. The secondary also provided strong coverage.

"It was a combination of both," Patterson said. "We used zone blitzes and we just rushed them. We wanted to make sure [Griffin] didn't hurt us with his legs. He did a little bit. He's just getting back in the swing of things [after a season-ending injury in 2009]. He's going to continue to get better."

Griffin's few big gains early came on the ground and were usually out of desperation. It wasn't until his 53-yard scoring strike late in the third that he had any success throwing deep.

But by then the outcome had all but been decided. The offense made sure of that.

"I think Andy called a great game," Patterson said. "It's really hard not to win the ballgame when you score that many points. When you put the ball in the end zone it's easy to play defense that way."

	1	2	3	4	T
Baylor	3	0	7	0	10
TCU	21	14	3	7	45

Wide receiver Jimmy Young races down field. Young's 29-yard reception in the first quarter set up TCU's third touchdown of the game. *Ron Jenkins, Star-Telegram*

TCU
ADAMS

TCU 41, SMU 24
September 24, 2010 • Dallas, Texas

TCU takes SMU's "best shot" to rule the Iron Skillet rivalry

By Stefan Stevenson

Coach Gary Patterson loves the mantra, "You just have to win by one point." He said it often leading up to the Horned Frogs' Friday night game with Metroplex rival SMU.

And after the fourth-ranked Frogs handed the Mustangs a 41-24 defeat in front of a standing-room only crowd of 35,481 at Gerald J. Ford Stadium, Patterson had the look of a coach who had just escaped with a one-point road victory.

In some respects, it indeed felt as if TCU escaped with a 17-point victory.

"We took our crosstown rivals' best shot," Patterson said. "That's an Auburn-Alabama from our perspective, two weeks in a row. We've got two private schools in the state that want to be us. All we need to worry about right now is to be 5-0."

TCU didn't take control of the game until Jeremy Kerley saved the day with an 83-yard kick-off return early in the second half that set up a touchdown. The return couldn't have come at a more crucial time. SMU had just taken the lead 17-14 after turning an Andy Dalton interception into a touchdown on the previous series. But Kerley's return to the 13 set up Dalton's 11-yard touchdown pass to Bart Johnson and TCU reclaimed the lead for good.

"We knew we had to come back out emotional, and I got some good blocks, and I was ready to read them," Kerley said. "I'm glad my teammates could look at me as kind of a leader to get a spark going, so it was no pressure on me. I just knew I had to go out there and do what I've been doing the last four years."

That swing of emotion took the wind out of the upset-minded Mustangs. And the TCU defense helped keep it deflated. The Frogs held SMU to 159 yards in the second half and were on the prowl for quarterback Kyle Padron the entire game.

They forced Padron to overthrow two passes on SMU's next series and TCU took over on its 42. Waymon James, subbing for Ed Wesley (who left in the first half with a concussion) capped a 12-play drive with a 9-yard touchdown to give TCU a 28-17 lead.

Bart Johnson and Jeremy Kerley celebrate in the end zone after Johnson's third-quarter touchdown catch that gave TCU a 21-17 lead.
Ronald Martinez, Getty Images

TCU
6
TCU
KERLEY
85
23

After another stand by the TCU defense, the offense put the game away with a six-play, 64-yard drive ending Luke Shivers' 4-yard run.

"It's basically the O-line," said Shivers, who has six scores in 10 career touches. "They do a good job and I just find the end zone. That's the easy part. I think that put us up by three possessions there, so it was a big touchdown for us."

Just like last season's game, SMU (2-2) struck first. The Mustangs took advantage of some gaping holes in the TCU defense early and running back Zach Line, who finished with a career-high 139 yard rushing, made the Frogs pay with 76 first-half yards. His running set up the Mustangs' first score, a 23-yard pass from Padron to Aldrick Robinson in the first quarter.

(above) A TCU cheerleader keeps the fans rooting for the Frogs. (opposite) Andy Dalton evades a tackle by SMU's Taylor Reed. Dalton passed for 174 yards and gained 43 more on the ground. *AP Images*

HORNED FROGS
34

"You've got to give SMU credit," Patterson said. "They got ready to play. They were physical. They got ready to go. We took their best shot and came out with a victory."

The TCU defense asserted itself on SMU's second series, putting the pressure on Padron and forcing the Mustangs into their second consecutive punt. Padron was hit hard several times on the series, with Tank Carder leveling him on a deep pass attempt to Robinson.

The Mustangs drove to the TCU 43, but Wayne Daniels and D.J. Yendrey combined to stop Line for a 2-yard loss. Stansly Maponga then pummeled Padron on third-and-8, forcing a fumble, which SMU recovered.

The Frogs took over on their 30 after a 15-yard punt. Dalton led a 15-play, 70-yard drive that included two fourth-down conversions and TCU took a 14-7 lead.

Wesley was injured on the drive when he tried to reverse field on third-and-4. He lost two yards, but on a fourth-down play from the SMU 29, Dalton connected with Johnson on a crossing pattern for seven yards for a first down.

Shivers then caught a rollout pass in the right flat to pick up nine yards on a fourth down to the SMU 5, and James scored from the 4 to make it 14-7.

	1	2	3	4	T
TCU	7	7	14	13	41
SMU	7	3	7	7	24

Jake Kirkpatrick holds up the Iron Skillet trophy as he and teammates celebrate after TCU's 41-24 win over SMU. *AP Images*

HORNED FRO
Mtn. WEST

TCU 27, Colorado State 0
October 2, 2010 • Fort Collins, Colorado

The defense shines, but offense takes a while

By Stefan Stevenson

Coach Gary Patterson had a simple order for his offense before the second half kickoff Saturday at Hughes Stadium.

"You're the No. 5 team in the nation," Patterson exclaimed in a huddle before the Horned Frogs took the field. "Play like it."

The plea woke up his sluggish offense. Five plays later, the Frogs scored their first touchdown against Colorado State en route to a 27-0 victory in their Mountain West Conference opener.

It was the first road shutout for TCU in Patterson's 10 years as head coach. And with the offense struggling to put up points in the first half, the Frogs needed a top defensive performance.

"We played a lot better defensively today," Patterson said. "When you go on the road, it's hard to do that. It's good for those kids; they're the ones who do all the hard work. Defensively, we're very happy with where we're at right now."

TCU (5-0, 1-0 MWC) outgained Colorado State 474 yards to 161 but struggled to put the ball in the end zone. TCU led 6-0 at the half on two field goals by Ross Evans.

Despite the offensive ineptitude, the Frogs' defense made it seem as if TCU led 60-0. TCU held the Rams to 51 total yards and two first downs in the first half. Part of the Rams' struggles was due to the loss of running back Raymond Carter in the first quarter because of a knee injury. The Rams were also without injured offensive tackle Mark Starr.

But the real reason for TCU's dominance might have been its less-than-sterling performance against SMU last week. The Frogs' defense allowed 24 points and 361 yards to the Mustangs, and Patterson, while crediting SMU's offense, was embarrassed.

"Every game we're trying to pitch a shutout, so it's easy for the offense to win," said Tanner Brock, who finished with a team-high 10 tackles. "We had something to prove after last week when we gave up too many yards rushing, and I think we went out there and did that today."

The Rams were held to 45 yards rushing, and

Andy Dalton looks to pass during the first quarter. He completed 11 passes for 109 yards and netted 67 yards on the ground to lead the Frogs to a 27-0 win. *Jack Dempsey, AP Images*

schutt
Mtn. West
HORNED FROGS
14

quarterback Pete Thomas was sacked four times.

"It's awesome to have a defense like ours," said Andy Dalton, who set a TCU record with his 50th touchdown pass, a 39-yard toss to Jimmy Young in the fourth quarter. "To hold them to a shutout is pretty tough to do."

Dalton didn't have a particularly good day passing (11-of-24 for 109 yards), but his receivers didn't do much to help, especially early. They dropped five passes, including four on the Frogs' opening drive. The Frogs moved the ball on the drive but had to settle for a 29-yard field goal.

TCU put together another drive at the end of the first quarter but stalled at the Rams' 26, resulting in an Evans 43-yard field goal. The offense was then forced to punt on its last three possessions of the half.

"The first rule of offensive football is don't stop yourself," Patterson said. "We were stopping ourselves. You don't have the [home] crowd around you

(above) Tanner Brock (35) and Greg McCoy take down a Colorado State ball carrier during the third quarter. The Frogs limited their opponent to just 161 yards total offense. (opposite) Colorado State wide receiver Lou Greenwood is taken down by TCU's Tanner Brock (35) and Jason Teague (27). *AP Images*

TCU
35
Colorado State

and all those things that get you hyped up before a game. You've got to be able to do it for yourself, and we didn't do a good job of that early in the game."

With the defense holding firm, the offense came alive in the second half. The Frogs drove 80 yards in two minutes, 20 seconds to take a 13-0 lead on Ed Wesley's 8-yard run. The score was set up by a 47-yard gallop by Matthew Tucker behind a big block by Luke Shivers, and Dalton's 16-yard run.

Later in the third quarter, Wesley scored on a 3-yard run behind the block of Marcus Cannon to give the Frogs a 20-0 cushion.

Patterson was happy his offense turned it on in the second half but warned that a similar performance against Air Force or Utah would not end well.

"Down the road, if we play that way in places like Utah, you're not going to win a conference title," said Patterson, who won his 90th game as head coach. "You have to pay attention to detail and score touchdowns, not field goals."

The Frogs rushed for a season-high 346 yards as Tucker (eight carries for 87 yards), Wesley (15 for 80) and Waymon James (6 for 55) each took turns bursting through big holes. Dalton began to use an effective read option more in the second half and finished with 67 yards rushing on 10 carries.

"We can run the football," Patterson said. "But we've got to score points. Yards don't make any difference. You've got to play in the red zone. They know they've got to play better."

	1	2	3	4	T
TCU	3	3	14	7	27
CS	0	0	0	0	0

Colorado State safety Ezra Thompson looks on as TCU's Ed Wesley rushes into the end zone. Wesley scored two touchdowns on the day. *AP Images*

TCU
34
13

Evan Frosch

TCU tight end is more than just an extra lineman

By Stefan Stevenson

Evan Frosch didn't know it while growing up in Midland, but there were signs pointing him in the direction of TCU.

The senior tight end's last name means "Frog" in German, and his parents decorated the Frosch family home with little frog ornaments.

Frosch's size and athletic ability also had something to do with him becoming a Horned Frog in 2006. At 6-foot-4 and 265 pounds, he played four years of basketball at Midland Lee and starred on the football team at linebacker and tight end.

By his senior season Frosch had focused on offense, but he was still listed as a linebacker in Dave Campbell's Texas Football's 2005 super list. He was also a Rivals-ranked recruit at tight end.

"I liked defense a lot, but I came here for tight end," said Frosch, 22.

Unlike last year, Frosch's longtime roommate and quarterback, Andy Dalton, is using his backs and tight ends more in the offense. Through seven games Dalton has connected with them 20 times, including seven completions to tight ends. Junior Logan Brock leads the team's tight ends with three receptions. Frosch and sophomore Corey Fuller each have two catches. Through seven games last season, Brock and Frosch had five catches and finished the season with eight.

"We've been getting more looks lately than we did then," said Frosch, who said he occasionally needles Dalton for more throws. "He's been trying to get us the ball."

Logan Brock, the older brother of linebacker Tanner Brock, said catching passes is a thrill, but he knows blocking up front helps the team just as much.

"It's a lot of fun for us, a little change of pace, but for us tight ends, it's always whatever we can do to help the team," Brock said. "We don't get a whole lot of glory, but that's all right with us as long as we're helping the team doing our job. But we do appreciate Andy showing us some love out there."

That seemed in jeopardy earlier in the season after two of Dalton's four interceptions came on

Offensive tackle Zach Roth (left) and tight end Evan Frosch unload frozen turkeys at a local food bank. A grocery store chain donates turkeys for every point TCU's high-octane offense scores. *Max Faulkner, Star-Telegram*

WIN #4
TCU FOOTBALL
MAKE IT HAPPEN
TURKEY
TURKEY

passes intended for tight ends. But Dalton was mistake-free in the first three games of October against Colorado State, Wyoming, and BYU.

He's completed 13 passes to backs and tight ends in those three games. The Frogs have even employed three-tight end sets at times this season, including using tight ends in the backfield to give defenses another wrinkle to worry about.

"They use us for all sorts of stuff, which is nice," Frosch said. "We take pride in our blocking. We consider ourselves dual threats being able to catch the ball."

Frosch and Dalton have been roommates since arriving on campus in the summer 2006. Center Jake Kirkpatrick lived with them until he got married in June 2009.

"We tried to get him to stay, but he said he had to go," Frosch joked. "We like [Jake's wife] Callie so much we thought it'd be nice if she was rooming with us, too. It was sad to see him go."

Frosch and Dalton will often spend nights watching game replays, usually fast-forwarding through the defense and dissecting the offense play by play.

"We'll sit there and rewind it and watch each play four or five times, looking at different people," Frosch said. "A lot of it's funny stuff like, 'Look at Jake, he threw somebody down.' Sometimes it's looking at coverage and wishing we had run this or that play because the defense did something."

Frosch graduated in December with a communications degree and a minor in business.

"He does all the right things, all the little details," Brock said.

And that includes embracing the grunt work of blocking. As a result, the tight ends have been allowed into the sacred, inner sanctum of the offensive line.

"I've always viewed myself as a glorified offensive tackle," Brock said. "Most times it's just blocking and I've embraced that. I love blocking. Most of my best friends are offensive linemen. I feel real comfortable with them." ■

Evan Frosch races down field on his 31-yard reception in the first quarter of TCU's Sept. 24 win over SMU. *AP Images*

84
Mtn. West

TCU 45, Wyoming 0
October 09, 2010 • Fort Worth, Texas

Frogs dominate Wyoming, earn second straight shutout

By Stefan Stevenson

Last year's TCU football team set all sorts of milestones on its way to the school's first BCS bowl game.

Historic offensive numbers. The top-ranked defense in the nation. And the most regular-season wins in Horned Frogs history.

But those Frogs never had back-to-back shutouts.

Fifth-ranked TCU earned consecutive shutouts for the first time in 55 years with a dominating 45-0 victory over Wyoming on Saturday before a crowd of 38,081 at Amon G. Carter Stadium. TCU (6-0, 2-0 Mountain West Conference) shut out Colorado State 27-0 last week.

Struggling BYU (2-4, 1-1), which defeated San Diego State on Saturday, visits Fort Worth this week. The Cougars changed defensive coordinators last week after giving up more than 400 yards per game.

Defense has not been an issue for the Frogs.

TCU's defense, ranked third in the nation, held Wyoming (2-4, 0-2) to 191 yards and eight first downs. That's the third time this season the Frogs have held opponents to less than 200 yards. Last year's team did it five times in 13 games.

"It's cool," TCU coach Gary Patterson said. "But, for me, I go back to the 'W'. I was excited for our kids. More and more they're doing a lot better job on the sideline with making adjustments."

Patterson credited the Frogs offense for also helping with the shutout. TCU gained 578 yards and kept the Wyoming offense, which was without starting quarterback Austyn Carta-Samuels, off the field. The Cowboys only ran 45 plays, giving the TCU defense plenty of time to reload and energize.

After the Frogs scored their final touchdown in the first minute of the fourth quarter, reserves filled out the lineup on both sides of the ball.

Midway through the fourth, the Cowboys drove 54 yards to the TCU 13-yard line, but Tyler Luttrell, back at strong safety after suffering an injury in Week 1, intercepted a Dax Crum pass at the 4-yard line.

Tekerrein Cuba, who has started the past two games at weak safety for the injured Alex Ibiloye,

Jeremy Kerley hauls in TCU's first touchdown against Wyoming, a 50-yard reception. *AP Images*

NIKE
85

was relieved. Four plays earlier he was beaten for a 39-yard pass to put the shutout in jeopardy.

"It was like a big weight lifted off my shoulder because I got beat on the previous play," Cuba said. "I congratulated [Luttrell] and thanked him for that."

But Cuba played well, otherwise, leading the Frogs with 12 tackles.

Wyoming's offense, which ran three successful trick plays last week, used another one on its opening play from scrimmage. Crum connected with Travis Burkhalter for 40 yards on a reverse-turned lateral pass-turned bomb.

But the Cowboys only gained 151 yards the rest of the game and entered TCU territory just three times. TCU made Wyoming pay on a fake punt attempt on the Cowboys' 36 at the end of the first quarter. Senior cornerback Malcolm Williams

(above) Wyoming running back Alvester Alexander loses his helmet as he is taken down by TCU defenders Joseph Bates and Travaras Battle. *Ron T. Ennis, Star-Telegram* (opposite) TCU quarterback Andy Dalton attempts to dive beyond the grasp of Wyoming defender Shamiel Gary. Dalton rushed for 42 yards on the day. *Richard W. Rodriguez, Special to the Star-Telegram*

TCU
14

stayed home on a direct snap to Tashaun Gipson, who gained just a yard before Williams brought him down. Two plays later Bart Johnson scored on a 31-yard pass from Andy Dalton to make it 21-0.

TCU scored on five of six first-half possessions, with the last one ending at midfield when time expired. The dominance resumed in the second half, as TCU scored touchdowns on long drives of 5:09 and 6:04. Matthew Tucker scored on a 5-yard run and Antoine Hicks scored on a 4-yard pass to start the fourth quarter to end the scoring and bring in the reserves.

"We were able to execute well and we just kept rolling with it," said Dalton, who completed 14 of 17 passes for 270 yards and three touchdowns. "The one drive we didn't score a touchdown [and settled for a field goal] we hurt ourselves with penalties."

Dalton and the offense mixed it up well. His first seven completions were to different receivers. Eight running backs touched the ball.

Ed Wesley finished with 115 yards rushing, his third 100-yard game of the season. Wesley provided one of the game's many highlights with a 17-yard touchdown run in which he broke the grasp of a defender, spun around, broke another tackle and busted in for the score.

"It was a fun day," said Patterson, who said he did not know how long it had been since TCU pitched consecutive shutouts. "If I get beat by BYU next week, no one will care."

	1	2	3	4	T
Wyoming	0	0	0	0	0
TCU	14	17	7	7	45

Andy Dalton dives for first down yardage early in the game. TCU's shutout of Wyoming marked the first time in 55 years that the Frogs blanked two consecutive opponents. *Ron T. Ennis, Star-Telegram*

TCU
DALTON
14

TCU 31, BYU 3
October 16, 2010 • Fort Worth, Texas

TCU offense ends first half with a flurry

By Stefan Stevenson

TCU didn't get its third consecutive shutout, but the Horned Frogs' defense was about as dominant as it's ever been.

The Horned Frogs broke open a tight game with two touchdowns just before the half and held BYU to 147 total yards to win 31-3 Saturday in front of 40,416 at Amon G. Carter Stadium.

The Frogs' top-ranked defense, which was working on 10 consecutive scoreless quarters, finally permitted a 27-yard field goal with 1 minute, 14 seconds remaining in the third quarter.

By then TCU had built a 17-0 lead. The offense, which has made a habit of running through, around and over opponents this season, found itself in a brawl with the Cougars through much of the first half. BYU consistently stuffed the run, so Andy Dalton and the offense took to the air.

After the defense stopped BYU deep in its own territory, Dalton took advantage of great field position at the Cougars' 46. He connected with Josh Boyce for two passes, the second a 35-yard touchdown over the middle to give the Frogs a 10-0 lead with 1:30 left in the half.

Two plays later on BYU's next possession, Tank Carder intercepted a Jake Heaps pass at the BYU 38, giving TCU's offense a chance to add to the lead. Dalton hit Bart Johnson for a 23-yard gain before tossing a 14-yard touchdown pass to Jimmy Young for a 17-0 lead with 0:26 left in the half.

"It was big," TCU coach Gary Patterson said. "You get some points on the board. [BYU] was playing it close to the vest, keeping it close. To be able to get those two scores, I thought, was really big for us."

TCU (7-0, 3-0 in the Mountain West) rushed for a season-low 108 yards on 38 carries, but Dalton made up for it with a season-high 273 yards passing and four touchdowns.

"They had some bigger guys up front, and for whatever reason we couldn't get some movement," Dalton said of the Frogs' rushing struggles. "We just relied on the passing game a little bit more and took what they gave us."

Andy Dalton looks downfield during the fourth quarter against BYU. Dalton passed for 273 yards and four touchdowns.
Sharon Ellman, Special to the Star-Telegram

schutt
14
FROGS
CUTTERS

After going scoreless in the third quarter, Dalton led the Frogs on two touchdown drives to start the fourth. Boyce took a pass on the sideline and ran in for a 20-yard touchdown to cap an eight-play, 64-yard drive to make it 24-3. On their next possession the Frogs were looking at a fourth-and-3 at the BYU 21 with 4:30 remaining. TCU went for it, and when Dalton's safe option didn't materialize, he found Jeremy Kerley in the corner of the end zone for a 21-yard touchdown.

"We were just trying to get a first down and run the clock," said Dalton, who completed 24 of 36 passes. "They covered it and Kerley got open and he made a good catch."

BYU (2-5, 1-2), trying to turn around its season, came out early and stifled the Frogs' rushing attack, which had averaged nearly 280 yards per game this

(above) TCU freshman defensive end Stansly Maponga sacks BYU quarterback Jake Heaps during the second quarter. (opposite) Ed Wesley finds daylight, eluding a BYU defender. Wesley gained 53 yards on 10 carries. *Sharon Ellman, Special to the Star-Telegram*

TCU
34

season. A muffed snap on the Frogs' first possession led to the first of six TCU punts.

"Finally we got going and we got rolling a little bit," Dalton said. "We had the big interception by Tank and that gave us a little momentum and we went down and scored again."

The Frogs defense, which entered the game ranked No. 1 in the nation after two consecutive shutouts, was more than up to the task. TCU held BYU to 13 yards and one first down in the first half. BYU's 147 total yards represent the Cougars' lowest offensive output since Utah held them to 156 in 2003. It's also the lowest total by a TCU opponent since San Diego State was held to 87 yards on Oct. 4, 2008.

Safety Tejay Johnson, who intercepted Heaps in the third quarter, says the defense has improved from each game to the next.

"It's exciting to see our defense progressing and really starting to play together," said Johnson, who has six career interceptions. "We really started seeing it click today. I feel like we've grown and improved since the beginning of the year.

"There's always room to get better."

Asked whether he's ever coached a defense playing such a dominant streak of football, Patterson demurred.

"Not that I remember, but we've played some awfully good defense here before," he said. "The last three weeks we've played young quarterbacks. I'm not ready to vote them the next Pittsburgh Steelers [Steel Curtain] yet." ■

	1	2	3	4	T
BYU	0	0	3	0	3
TCU	3	14	0	14	31

Jeremy Kerley breaks past BYU defenders on a first-quarter punt return. *Sharon Ellman, Special to the Star-Telegram*

TCU
85

Tejay Johnson

Coach Gary Patterson calls safety a "glue guy"

By Stefan Stevenson

Leading comes easy for Tejay Johnson. As the oldest of 11 brothers and sisters, Johnson assumes the role naturally.

His leadership skills have been on display since his freshman season in 2007.

TCU coach Gary Patterson doesn't hand over the keys to his defense to just anybody. So choosing Johnson to represent the vaunted Horned Frogs' defense–which has led the nation statistically the past two seasons–at the Mountain West Conference Media Days is quite the honor.

"It means a lot to be here representing the TCU defense," said Johnson, who had 59 tackles and three interceptions in 2009. Especially when Johnson is reminded of some of the former Frogs who have been here in the past such as Jerry Hughes, David Hawthorne and Jeremy Modkins.

"Just to be in that category is an honor because I know the kind of players they were," he said.

For all his natural athletic skill–quickness to the ball, and power and strength to take down bigger opponents–it's Johnson's intelligence that has allowed Patterson to entrust him with quarterbacking the secondary.

"He's one of our glue guys on defense," Patterson said to the gathered media. "He tells everyone what to do."

Johnson does more than help out teammates in the heat of the moment on Saturdays. In the summer, he tutored freshmen (and a few older players) on the Frogs' 4-2-5 scheme by breaking down film for them and going over different looks.

"I sort of picked up from coach that you learn it on the board and then you have to take it to the field," said Johnson, who also has helped run defensive drills this summer. "You can teach it to them on the board and they'll get it, but when you get them on the field and they're in the situation it turns in to chaos because they don't know what's going on."

The easiest way for players to learn the Frogs' defense is to only worry about their job, said Johnson, no doubt echoing the sentiment bellowed from defensive coaches during his career.

"Most young players try to look at too much," he said. "If you look at what you're supposed to do, I feel like it's pretty simple to pick up on."

Part of the learning curve comes from the type of defense most players saw in high school.

"Most of the safeties played deep in high school so they could see what all was going on, but in this defense you have to be run-oriented and pass-oriented at the same time," Johnson said. "At the college level things happen so much quicker you don't have time to think and look around and then react."

Growing up with four sisters and six brothers didn't leave Johnson much time to react to anything. He became the first from his family to attend college. He's set to graduate in May with a degree in habilitation of the deaf and hard of hearing. ■

Tejay Johnson, left, and Tank Carder spin on the Mad Tea Party ride at Disneyland. TCU and Wisconsin players visited the theme park on Dec. 26, 2010, before the teams' Rose Bowl matchup six days later. *AP Images*

ANAHEIM
VIZIO
TCU

TCU 38, Air Force 7
October 23, 2010 • Fort Worth, Texas

Ed Wesley's career day outdoes Falcons' option by himself

By Stefan Stevenson

TCU's defense gave all due respect to Air Force's triple-option running game this week. TCU coach Gary Patterson and his players said all the right things about what it would take to shut the Falcons' top-ranked rushing game down.

On Saturday night, they put those words into action.

The fourth-ranked Horned Frogs held Air Force to 184 rushing yards—162.9 yards below its average —and pulled away in the second half to win 38-7.

The Frogs, who are ranked No. 5 in the BCS standings, showcased their rushing game before a crowd of 46,096 at Amon G. Carter Stadium. It was the fifth-largest crowd in the stadium's history. The Frogs only have one home game left—Nov. 14 against San Diego State—before a massive renovation begins at the stadium.

Ed Wesley rushed for a career-high 209 yards, single-handedly outgaining the nation's best rushing team, as the Frogs totaled 377 yards on the ground. The Frogs scored on runs from Wesley, who had two touchdowns, Andy Dalton and Matthew Tucker. Dalton also connected with Jeremy Kerley for an 8-yard touchdown pass just before halftime.

Wesley's 209 yards are the most by a Frogs running back since Joseph Turner gained 226 yards at San Diego State in 2007.

"Gosh," Dalton gushed when asked about Wesley. "To see what he did tonight was impressive. He's playing with unbelievable passion this year."

Dalton had a big night rushing, too, including a dash for 47 yards in the second half.

"I've never seen that much open grass in my life," Dalton said.

Dalton finished with a career-high 93 yards rushing and 185 yards passing.

"It's one of our complete efforts," said TCU coach Gary Patterson, who credited the offense for keeping the Falcons off the field.

After a tight first quarter ended tied at 7-7, the Frogs (8-0, 4-0 Mountain West Conference) began to wear down the Falcons (5-3, 3-2).

Ed Wesley dodges Air Force defenders Anthony Wooding Jr. (34) and Jon Davis (6) en route to one of his two touchdowns on the day.
Sharon Ellman, Special to the Star-Telegram

DAVIS
6
34

Before halftime, TCU scored twice to take a 17-7 lead. Ross Evans kicked a 30-yard field goal to make it 10-7 and the defense stuffed Air Force on four plays with three minutes remaining in the half. From their own 11, the Frogs drove nine plays for a touchdown, as Wesley's legs willed the offense down the field. He had runs of 9, 7 and 22 yards on the drive. Dalton connected with Antoine Hicks for 38 yards and capped it off with an 8-yard touchdown strike in the corner of the end zone to Kerley with 16 seconds left in the half.

"That changed the makeup of the ballgame," Patterson said. "I think it was big to go up by scores."

TCU fans will be curious to see where the Frogs move in today's updated Bowl Championship Series standings. The Frogs are ranked No. 5 this week but after No. 1 Oklahoma lost at Missouri there should be major shuffling.

(above) Ed Wesley celebrates with teammates after one of his two touchdowns. (opposite) Wesley carries Air Force defenders Anthony Wooding Jr. and Jon Davis into the end zone. *Sharon Ellman, Special to the Star-Telegram*

TCU
TCU
TCU
DAVIS
6
6

"The last three times we've been down here, they've been dominant," Air Force coach Troy Calhoun said. "Right now there's a gap. That's stating the obvious."

Calhoun was likely just talking about a gap between TCU and Air Force, but the Frogs are showing a gap between themselves and the entire Mountain West Conference. A huge battle looms in two weeks when the Frogs travel to No. 9 Utah. In its first four league games the Frogs have outscored their opponents 141 to 10. The Falcons' first-quarter touchdown was the first touchdown allowed by TCU in October.

"Every challenge I've asked this team to do they've stepped to this year," Patterson said of his team's effort Saturday. "Air Force is a tough football team. You've got to play fast. If you don't understand their movement then you're in a lot of trouble."

But after allowing 73 first-quarter rushing yards, the Frogs defense turned it up a notch, holding the Falcons to 111 yards on the ground the last three quarters.

"They play fast and we had to adjust to the game," said safety Colin Jones. "It was in the back of our minds that we wanted to go out there and show what we could do [against the Air Force rushing game]."

	1	2	3	4	T
Air Force	7	0	0	0	7
TCU	7	10	14	7	38

Running back Matthew Tucker scores on a six-yard run in the third quarter to give TCU a 31-7 lead. *Sharon Ellman, Special to the Star-Telegram*

TCU
29

TCU 48, UNLV 6

October 30, 2010 • Las Vegas, Nevada

Frogs dominate despite fumbles

By Stefan Stevenson

The postgame celebration in the TCU locker room after its 48-6 shellacking of UNLV late Saturday night was nothing more than a quick chant and a prayer. And then the Horned Frogs' focus was turned exclusively to Utah.

The fourth-ranked Horned Frogs didn't play their cleanest game of the season Saturday night in front of a paltry 16,745 in attendance at Sam Boyd Stadium, but they still came away with the same predictable victory that has been the norm during league play this season. TCU has outscored Mountain West opponents 189-16. The win sets up a MWC showdown Saturday in Salt Lake City with the Frogs traveling for a meeting with No. 8 Utah.

It would not be hyperbolic to say that not only does the MWC title rest on the outcome, but also the BCS bowl aspirations for both schools.

TCU has never beaten Utah in Salt Lake City. The last meeting there was on a Thursday night in 2008. The then No.9-ranked Utes scored a touchdown in the final minute to win 13-10 to preserve their perfect record. Utah finished undefeated and beat Alabama in the Sugar Bowl. TCU was No. 11 at the time and finished 11-2 and beat Boise State in the Poinsettia Bowl.

Both Utah (8-0, 5-0) and TCU (9-0, 5-0) will likely be ranked in the top seven of the new BCS standings, which will be announced at 7:15 p.m. Sunday on ESPN. This week TCU is No. 4 and Utah is No. 8.

"People know about Utah and people know about TCU," Frogs' coach Gary Patterson said. "You wouldn't want it any different. You always like it when you're playing for a championship. We understand what kind of football team they have and how talented they are."

Any idea that TCU would overlook the struggling Rebels Saturday night was disproven early. The Frogs scored on their first possession–a 5-yard run by Jeremy Kerley–to cap a 10-play, 64-yard drive. TCU took a 14-0 lead to start the second quarter on Ed Wesley's 1-yard run, which capped an eight-play, 60-yard drive.

Jeremy Kerley tries to move past a UNLV defender. Kerley totaled five catches for 82 yards and a touchdown. *AP Images*

REBELS
91
REBELS
REBELS

Meanwhile, the Frogs' defense forced two punts on the Rebels' first two possessions which netted five total yards. Colin Jones returned an interception 30 yards for a touchdown on the Rebels' third possession to make it 21-0.

"I didn't think we played that well on both sides of the ball but we did what we needed to do," said Patterson, who declined to let any TCU players speak to the media. He said the team was in a hurry to get back to its hotel. Patterson wanted his team to get a good night's sleep instead of flying back after the game.

"Last time we got back late and had to play a Thursday night game," said Patterson, recalling a late game at UNLV in 2008 the week before playing at Utah. "So we're trying to give ourselves the best opportunity to be successful."

The Frogs outgained the Rebels 530 to 197 but fumbled three times, including one by Matthew Tucker at the goal line.

The Rebels offense put together one impressive drive, going 75 yards on nine plays to score its only touchdown of the night, a 10-yard pass to Michael Johnson from Omar Clayton. The initial extra point was good but the Rebels (1-7, 1-3) were called for holding and missed the second chance.

But the Frogs defense, overall, remained in a dominating zone, and clamped down the rest of the way. The Rebels were forced to punt six times and had just 81 yards after scoring their second-quarter touchdown.

The Rebels attempted a fake punt from the Frogs 47 but punter Brendon Lamers pass to Mike Grant was short and the Frogs took over with 3:33 left in the half. TCU took advantage with a quick

Andy Dalton celebrates after a second-quarter touchdown. Dalton's 1-yard run gave the Frogs a 28-6 lead heading into halftime. *AP Images*

TCU
14

eight-play, 53-yard scoring drive. Andy Dalton scored on a 1-yard run with a minute left before halftime to give TCU a 28-6 lead.

In the second half, Dalton helped break it open with a 54-yard touchdown pass to Josh Boyce, who galloped untouched from the 30-yard line after his defender had fallen down. Dalton also connected with Kerley for a 24-yard touchdown to make it 42-6 early in the fourth quarter.

Ed Wesley led the Frogs with 64 yards on 13 carries. Waymon James and Aundre Dean, who played most of the fourth quarter, finished with 61 and 47 yards, respectively. Dalton finished with 252 yards passing after completing 16 of 23 attempts passes and two touchdowns. Redshirt freshman Casey Pachall, who played much of the fourth quarter for Dalton, scored his first career touchdown on an eight-yard run with 4:10 remaining. The Frogs had a chance to add more points late in the game after Dean broke around the right side for 35 yards to the 11 with 2:00 remaining, but the Frogs took a knee three consecutive plays to run out the clock.

"We didn't need to score anymore points," Patterson said. "I'm always going to do it [that way]. We go about our business with class and always have and always will."

	1	2	3	4	T
TCU	7	21	7	13	48
UNLV	0	6	0	0	6

Jeremy Kerley scampers for a first down in the first quarter.
AP Images

HORNED FROGS
85

Jeremy Kerley

Hutto-born and bred, the Horned Frogs receiver is a star

By Stefan Stevenson

There's a Kerley Drive in Hutto. The street in Hutto, which is about 10 miles east of Round Rock and 30 miles northeast of Austin, isn't named after TCU's Jeremy Kerley.

Not specifically, anyway. Not yet.

Hutto, which had a population of around 630 when Kerley was born in 1989, has become one of the fastest growing cities in America in recent years, ballooning to more than 17,000 as urban sprawl inches north from Austin.

Kerley barely recognizes the town when he makes it back to visit family, which has deep roots in the community that date back a century. Kerley Drive was named after a great-grandfather from a generation ago.

"If you're driving through Hutto and sneeze, you're going to miss it," said Kerley, who still can't help but think of the town as it was when he was a youngster turning heads on athletic fields.

By the time Kerley entered Hutto High School, he was the most well-known athlete in town. But when he was selected the Hippos' starting varsity quarterback as a freshman, it took most by surprise.

Even the Hippos' new offensive coordinator at the time, Mickey Bushong, questioned head coach Lee Penland.

"I got to Hutto and they tell me some little freshman kid is going to be my quarterback," said Bushong, who had come to the 1-9 Hippos from Austin Reagan. "And he'd never played quarterback."

Penland told Bushong to give the kid a look.

"He may be a little different than most other freshmen," Penland told him.

Two days into August two-a-days, Bushong pulled Penland aside.

"You know what, I think we're going to be all right with this Kerley kid," he told Penland.

Kerley helped lead Hutto to its first state championship game his junior season in 2005. The Hippos lost to Tatum 38-34 in the middle game of a triple header at Texas Stadium.

A red-haired quarterback from Katy named Andy Dalton had faced Southlake Carroll in a Class 5A championship in the early game.

"He's probably the most athletic guy I've ever been around," said Dalton, who teamed up with Kerley at TCU as freshmen in 2007. "He does everything." ■

Jeremy Kerley, from the small Texas town of Hutto, has made it big on the national stage. *Brandon Wade, Special to the Star-Telegram*

Mtn. WEST
TCU
HORNED FROGS
85

TCU 47, Utah 7

November 6, 2010 • Salt Lake City, Utah

The rout in a matchup of BCS 3 vs. 5 clears the way

By Stefan Stevenson

In a season filled with dominating TCU wins, none was more impressive—or dominating—than the Horned Frogs' victory Saturday.

Fourth-ranked TCU, playing in the program's biggest regular-season game in five decades, manhandled sixth-ranked Utah 47-7 before the second-largest crowd ever (46,522) at Rice-Eccles Stadium. It was the fourth-biggest loss in Utes history and snapped their 21-game home winning streak. The victory boosted TCU's BCS-busting drive as emphatically as it ended Utah's.

"They put themselves on a different plateau," TCU coach Gary Patterson said he told his team after the win. "But they have to finish the season. I thought they made a statement today. Everybody else in the country [this season] that has gone into somebody else's house in a big ballgame has usually gotten beat. We'll see if we can win the next two weeks. Then we can have a conversation [about the BCS]."

The Frogs (10-0, 6-0 Mountain West Conference) host San Diego State on Saturday in the final game at Amon G. Carter Stadium before a major renovation gets under way. After an off week, TCU finishes at New Mexico on Nov. 27.

"We got another game to play," said Patterson, who championed San Diego State as a team on the rise. "It's our last home game for our seniors; they're tearing down Amon G. Carter Stadium. There's all kinds of things going on."

But there was no bigger collection of distractions and obstacles facing the Frogs than in Utah. With ESPN's College GameDay in town, the Frogs were trying to win at a place they'd never won before.

Instead of wilting under the intense spotlight, TCU, led by quarterback Andy Dalton, took command on its opening possession. The Frogs marched 80 yards and scored on Dalton's 26-yard touchdown pass to Josh Boyce.

The Frogs' defense, ranked No. 1 nationally for much of the season, forced eight punts and didn't

Linebacker Tanner Brock takes down Utah wide receiver Jereme Brooks during the first half. The Frogs held the fifth-ranked Utes scoreless for the first three quarters. *AP Images*

35

allow Utah (8-1, 5-1) beyond the 50-yard line until a fourth-quarter drive netted the Utes their only score of the game.

By then Dalton and the offense had built a 40-point lead. Dalton threw for a career-high 355 yards and three touchdowns. Receiver Jeremy Kerley threw his first-career touchdown, a 26-yard pass to Bart Johnson.

TCU's defensive line only registered one sack, but was a constant threat to Utah quarterback Jordan Wynn. If it wasn't Wayne Daniels (one sack, forced fumble) coming from the right edge, it was Stansly Maponga coming from the left edge. Or it was Tank Carder on a blitz. Wynn finished 16 of 35 passing for 148 yards with two interceptions, including one on the Utes' opening possession of the second half that Tanner Brock returned 57 yards to the Utes' 4.

(above) TCU coach Gary Patterson directs his team from the sideline. (opposite) Wide receiver Jimmy Young hauls in an 11-yard pass from Andy Dalton for a touchdown in the third quarter. *AP Images*

"I was surprised when I caught it because my hands are a little suspect at times," Brock joked. "I got a little tired when I got down near the end zone."

It set up a 4-yard touchdown run by Ed Wesley that gave the Frogs a 30-0 lead.

The Frogs had three one-play scoring drives in the game, including a 93-yard pass from Dalton to Boyce at the end of the first quarter.

"We knew the severity of this game," said senior Jimmy Young, who had five catches for 84 yards to move into fifth place all-time at TCU in receptions (136) and yards (2,161). "It was much more than a conference championship and coming to Utah and just getting a win."

Said Utah coach Kyle Whittingham: "The score was not indicative of how lopsided this game was. They were better at every phase of the game. We were outcoached and outplayed. Gary Patterson has something special there and they are an exceptionally high-quality football team."

How special they are and who they'll get to prove it against in the postseason is still in the hands of voters and computer rankings.

"To be able to put ourselves in a position to say we could play against anybody, we needed to do that against Utah today," Patterson said.

	1	2	3	4	T
TCU	20	3	14	10	47
Utah	0	0	0	7	7

Waymon James tries to shake off Utah cornerback Justin Taplin-Ross (33) during the second half of the Frogs' 47-7 win in Salt Lake City. *AP Images*

TCU
FROGS
HORNED FROGS
UTAH

TCU 40, San Diego State 35
November 13, 2010 • Fort Worth, Texas

Frogs rally in final home game before stadium renovation

By Stefan Stevenson

TCU coach Gary Patterson tried his best to put on a happy face after his Horned Frogs defeated San Diego State 40-35 on Saturday.

There should have been an overwhelming display of triumph from Patterson and his players during the postgame activities on the field and in the locker room after the third-ranked Frogs finished victorious in the final home game of 2010 and the last game at Amon G. Carter Stadium before the 80-year-old venue undergoes a massive renovation.

But that wasn't the case. Patterson tried to explain the dueling emotions swirling in his head after the Frogs (11-0, 7-0 Mountain West) prevailed where it mattered most—on the scoreboard—but may have failed to impress voters and computers enough to stay ahead of Boise State when today's Bowl Championship Series standings are announced.

"Bottom line, we found a way to win," Patterson said. "You have to give San Diego State a lot of credit."

The Aztecs quickly put TCU in unfamiliar territory by taking a 14-0 lead early in the game, sending an air of silence over the 45,694 in attendance. The Frogs hadn't trailed since early in the third quarter against SMU on Sept. 24.

Patterson compared the slow start to the Frogs' game at Wyoming last season after an emotional victory over Utah the previous week. Last year Wyoming hung with TCU for a quarter before Jeremy Kerley helped break it open with a 45-yard touchdown reception in the second quarter.

It was Kerley again Saturday who ignited the Frogs' comeback. His 38-yard touchdown reception on fourth-and-5 at the end of the first quarter ignited a 37-point outburst by TCU.

Patterson wasn't sure if his team was too tense or too loose, but there were plenty of distractions from which to choose. TCU was celebrating 26 seniors playing their last home game. There was the nostalgia of playing in Amon G. Carter Stadium for the last time before it's renovated.

Greg McCoy (7) and Tejay Johnson (3) celebrate McCoy's third-quarter interception. *Sharon Ellman, Special to the Star-Telegram*

TCU
HORNED FROGS
7
3
GSERIES

And then there was beloved offensive line coach Eddie Williamson, who suffered chest pains early in the first quarter. He was taken to Texas Health Harris Methodist Hospital Fort Worth, where he underwent angioplasty. His condition is stable, Patterson said.

When asked about the reasons for his team's slow start, Patterson said, "I don't know what they were. When I do, I'll write a book. Then I won't have to be standing up here in front of you guys telling you why I feel bad that we just won."

Patterson, as he had said all week, reiterated that San Diego State is a team on the rise.

"You have to go play this time of year in conference," he said. "Everybody is going to take their best shot. [San Diego State] did a great job of coming back and making it a ballgame."

The Aztecs (7-3, 4-2) used a flea-flicker to strike first on their opening three-play drive. Ryan Lindley connected with Vincent Brown for 49 yards to the Frogs' 1 to set up San Diego State's first score.

After punting on their first two possessions, the Frogs were backed up near their own goal line, where Andy Dalton was blindsided by the Aztecs' Rob Andrews. Dalton fumbled on the play and Jerome Long recovered it for a touchdown and a 14-0 lead.

But the Frogs finally got it together offensively on their next drive, moving 80 yards on 11 plays and ending with the first of Kerley's three touchdown receptions.

The Frogs held the Aztecs to one first down in the first half. San Diego State didn't make a second

Tanner Brock (35) puts a hit on San Diego State kickoff returner Brandon Davis. *Sharon Ellman, Special to the Star-Telegram*

35
11
TCU

first down until 2:10 was left in the third. Ross Evans missed two field goals and an extra point on the day, and the Frogs' offense again grew stagnant in the second half. In the final 6:43, the Aztecs scored twice on long touchdown passes from Lindley to Brown to put another scare into TCU.

"I know most of the team doesn't feel like we played to the best of our abilities," TCU safety Tejay Johnson said. "I think we kind of lost focus going into the fourth quarter and we had to find it."

TCU running backs Matthew Tucker and Waymon James, who rushed for 131 and 102 yards, respectively, were able to run out the final 4:42 to preserve the victory.

Patterson deflected questions about rankings and polls, while trying to remind everyone that his team is undefeated after 11 weeks.

"I can't do anything about the polls," he said. "It's not the kind of score we'd like to have, but it's a win. I should cheer up so everybody will be happy. We don't very often give up 35 points in this house. But the good part was we scored over 36. I'm pretty excited about that."

	1	2	3	4	T
SDS	14	0	7	14	35
TCU	13	21	3	3	40

Freshman wide receiver Josh Boyce tries to reel in a pass as the Aztecs' Josh Wade defends. *Sharon Ellman, Special to the Star-Telegram*

82

Williamson Not Afraid

TCU coach living life to the fullest

By Stefan Stevenson

When Patty Williamson finally made it to her husband's side, the first words out of TCU assistant coach Eddie Williamson's mouth were, "Did we score?"

The TCU Frog horn had just blown, and Williamson was lying on a table in the training room, oxygen mask on his face, having a heart attack.

It was early in the first quarter of the Horned Frogs' Nov. 13 game against San Diego State.

"I felt a little bit of tension or swelling in my chest," said Williamson, who felt fine during the coin toss and kickoff that day. "I thought I was just being emotional about senior day."

But during the Frogs' second offensive series, Williamson's arms began to go numb. Because of his CPR training, which is required of all TCU coaches, Williamson knew it was a sign of trouble. A trainer gave him a couple of aspirin, but the pain grew worse.

"I felt like I needed to get out of there and not let something happen on the sideline with the kids [present]," said Williamson, who calmly told co-offensive coordinator Jarrett Anderson he was leaving because "I think I'm having a heart attack."

Williamson walked with team doctor Sam Haraldson to the training room underneath Daniel-Meyer Coliseum behind the south end zone.

"It felt like an elephant was sitting on my chest," Williamson said. "It was actually getting that way on the sideline."

On the sidelines was Williamson's son, Eddie III, 29, who brought his 14-month-old son, Edwin Calvin Williamson IV, to the game. His grandson was in the stands with Patty, who didn't see her husband walk off the field, but soon received word.

"I was worried about my son, who was here with my grandson, who is a legacy and is named after me," Williamson said Saturday on his 59th birthday, his first day back coaching after successful emergency angioplasty to clear a lower artery that had become 80 to 85 percent blocked. A stint was inserted and Williamson was released from the hospital three days after the San Diego State game.

"I am a person of faith. I'm not afraid to die, but I didn't want to," Williamson said.

15 more minutes

It is not uncommon for coaches and others involved in high-stress athletics to suffer heart-related ailments, sometimes fatally. TCU football coach Jim Pittman suffered a fatal heart attack on the sidelines during a game against Baylor in 1971. In the locker room after an overtime win against

Offensive line coach Eddie Williamson patrols the sideline during TCU's game against SMU on Sept. 24. *AP Images*

TCU
TCU
86
84
12

Notre Dame on Sept. 18, Michigan State coach Mark Dantonio suffered a heart attack. Dantonio subsequently had angioplasty.

"The doctors were just amazing," said Patty, who has been married to Eddie for 31 years. "Just how quickly they took action; I think it was life-saving for him. They were so quick and attentive."

TCU doctors started monitoring Williamson's blood pressure and electrocardiogram in the training room. When Patty made it to his side, he asked about the score.

"Yes, we scored," she responded.

"So we're tied?" he asked.

"No, honey, we didn't get the extra point, so we're behind by one," she informed him as the Frogs trailed 14-13 at the end of the first quarter.

Soon he was placed in an ambulance and headed to Texas Health Harris Methodist Hospital in Fort Worth.

"It was a blessing I was where I was," said Eddie Williamson, who coaches the offensive line. "Because if I had stood there [on the field] another 15 minutes, I don't know if I'd be here today."

"Would you like to see a chaplain?"

Upon arriving at the emergency room, Williamson continued to ask for updates on the Frogs' game. He kept asking a nurse to check her iPhone for updates. The band of nurses kept asking the Williamsons if they'd like to see a chaplain or minister. They politely declined several times before Williamson said he didn't need a chaplain, but a doctor would be nice.

"He's a very committed Christian," Patty said. "He has a private devotional time every morning. His heart is fine with the Lord."

Nurses also kept asking if he was under stress, which struck Patty as comically absurd.

"My husband was on the sidelines of a nationally televised football game and we were losing," she said, pointing to the laminated sheet of plays still hanging from Williamson's belt loop. "Yes, he was under stress. Those are the plays TCU is running."

After a 90-minute procedure, Williamson was in the intensive-care unit recuperating and lamenting that the ER didn't have a television.

"They were ready for me," Williamson said. "I just kind of zipped through and got great care there. I was fortunate."

"After he was out of the procedure, I told my son, 'We aren't even going to talk about the game until it's over,'" Patty said. "I'm not going to tell them they've gotten close again."

The Aztecs outscored the Frogs 21-6 in the second half to close to five points late in the game, but TCU held on for a 40-35 victory.

15 large men are here

"You worry about your family," Williamson said of the initial thoughts swirling around his mind on the sidelines that day. "My wife is a strong woman. She was a real trouper, solid as a rock the whole time. After the initial deal, I was at complete peace with going to the hospital."

After the game, the offensive line gathered for an already planned cookout that turned into an impromptu prayer session for their coach. "It was like I was with my brothers, and we were praying for our dad," tackle Marcus Cannon said.

The next day, 15 offensive linemen crowded into Williamson's room in intensive care for an emotional meeting.

"They all filed past the nurses' station and surrounded his bed," Patty said. "It was a real emotional time for them and him. It was a very sweet time. They were just so concerned about him. They finally loosened up and told him about the game."

All-America center Jake Kirkpatrick said Williamson's absence that day was a shock. "When you look up to someone so much, when he's not there, it definitely feels like a void," said Kirkpatrick, who was in the room that next day. "He was tired, but he was happy to see us. He was joking around about needing to eat healthier. We were giving him a hard time about no Blue Bell [ice cream] for a while, just grilled chicken and vegetables for him."

"Those kids are like sons in a lot of ways," said Eddie Williamson, who invites the offensive line for dinner several times a year. "I appreciated the fact that they cared."

Not afraid to die

Williamson, an avid runner and weightlifter for most of his life, had worked out at the team hotel the morning of Nov. 13 and felt fine. He has lost 15 pounds since the episode and has cut his coffee consumption from eight cups a day to 1 ½ . TCU graduate assistant coaches were the recipients of the junk food cleared out of the Williamsons' kitchen, including the coach's beloved Blue Bell.

"I don't think people realize how hard these coaches work," said Patty, who moved her family 13 times in the first 20 years of the couple's 31-year marriage. "They get 4 ½ hours of sleep a night. They work seven days a week. They do not have days off. The human body can only take so much. The stress of the job and the stress of winning is heightened because they are so tired. It's just a fast and furious vocation."

Williamson is getting more rest now and is watching his diet closely. He will get to coach in the Rose Bowl on Jan. 1, something Patty believes was only possible because he took his recovery slowly. That wasn't easy for Williamson, who has missed only one day of work in 35 years, including the last 10 years at TCU. That was only after Patty refused to take him back to the office several years ago after he had knee surgery.

"I think the doctor figured out it was harder on his heart to leave him at home than it was to have him at the office or at the game," said TCU coach Gary Patterson, who hired Williamson to coach the offensive line in 2001. "The kids really like him, so to get him back part... has been a lot of fun."

Williamson now preaches to everyone to get a regular physical and "if you feel like something is happening, go to the doctor and find out.

"Don't play hero," Williamson said. "Let them tell you nothing is wrong."

He also learned a few things about himself. He had always joked that the best way to measure himself as a coach was if his unit was forced to play without his guidance. He hoped his players would know enough "about our system and our plan that even if we got in trouble they could get out of it.

"I didn't know I'd ever live it out that way, but that's really the truth," said Williamson, who told his players the story during their visit. "I thought they fought their way out of that mess pretty good that day."

"They were playing for themselves, but I think they were fighting for him, too," Patty said.

"The one thing I found out through all of this is I love life," Williamson said. "I want to stay alive, but I'm not afraid to die, either." ■

TCU 66, New Mexico 17
November 27, 2010 • Albuquerque, New Mexico

TCU races through the opening from Boise State's loss

By Stefan Stevenson

As usual, Andy Dalton was the last one off the field Saturday. The senior quarterback was the last one to squeeze into TCU's ecstatic locker room at University Stadium.

Dalton, excusing himself past TCU personnel, bowl representatives and reporters crowding the narrow hall leading into the locker room, made it in just as Mountain West Conference commissioner Craig Thompson awarded TCU the league's championship trophy after the Horned Frogs 66-17 thrashing of New Mexico.

But Dalton was already carrying TCU's even more impressive trophy—a long-stemmed rose.

TCU, ranked No. 3 in the Bowl Championship Series standings, is headed to the Rose Bowl in Pasadena, Calif., for the first time in school history after finishing undefeated for the second consecutive season. Boise State's overtime loss to Nevada on Friday night, Nov. 26, opened the door for TCU to remain ranked No. 3 in the BCS standings.

The top two teams—No. 1 Oregon and No. 2 Auburn—both won Friday, but both play regular-season finales next Saturday. Oregon is at Oregon State and Auburn meets South Carolina in the Southeastern Conference championship. If either team falters, the Frogs (12-0, 8-0 in Mountain West) could find themselves in the BCS National Championship Game on Jan. 10 in Glendale, Ariz. The bowl matchups are announced Dec. 5.

"I thought it was actually more pressure [for us]," said Patterson of Boise State's loss the night before. "You're playing for the chance to possibly go to the Rose or possibly play for the national championship if you can win out."

But TCU came out free and easy against New Mexico and built a 21-0 lead in the first eight minutes of the game on three touchdown passes by Dalton to wide-open receivers.

The Lobos (1-11, 1-7) scored two touchdowns in the first half after two TCU fumbles. New Mexico needed just 13 yards combined to convert the scores. The second fumble came when Dalton was

Ed Wesley carries the ball down field. The sophomore running back led the Frogs with 77 rushing yards on 11 carries. *AP Images*

schutt
HORNED FROG
34
70
LOBOS
EW MEXICO

knocked out of the remainder of the game on a sack.

His fumble on the play was returned 35 yards by Joe Stoner to the TCU 1-yard line. New Mexico made it 31-17 on Stump Godfrey's 1-yard run with 8:57 left in the first half.

After that, the TCU defense, which is trying to top the nation statistically for the third consecutive season, clamped down. TCU outgained the Lobos 503 to 130 yards and held a 24-9 first-down advantage.

Casey Pachall replaced Yogi Gallegos at quarterback after two series in the first half and finished the game for TCU. Dalton was hit on his elbow,

(above) Antoine Hicks scores on a 14-yard pass from Andy Dalton on the game's first drive. (opposite) New Mexico running back Kasey Carrier (21) tries to elude TCU defenders Clarence Leatch (95) and Johnny Fobbs (21) in the fourth quarter. *AP Images*

NEW MEXICO
TCU
21
21
TCU
95

which caused some numbness in his throwing arm. But he said he was OK near the end of the game.

In the second half, TCU ran the ball 27 times compared with five pass attempts, but the scoring continued for the Frogs.

After a New Mexico fumble, Pachall scored on an 8-yard run to the corner of the end zone. Less than two minutes later Curtis Clay's 50-yard punt return set up a 1-play scoring drive. Pachall hit Logan Brock in the flat and he raced in for a 21-yard touchdown to put the Frogs up 45-17.

TCU took advantage of great field position set up by defensive stands and long punt returns the entire game and added three short touchdown runs by Luke Shivers, Matthew Tucker and Aundre Dean.

"I told them at halftime this is not what we're about, the way we were acting," Patterson said of the first-half miscues. "Yeah, we lost our quarterback, but settle down and do what you're supposed to do. This group the last three years has been very workmanlike."

Now the Frogs must "wait and see what happens," Patterson said.

"It feels good to be winning and be a part of something like this," said Ed Wesley, who became TCU's first 1,000-yard rusher since 2003 with a team-leading 77 yards. "We're not sure where we're going to go."

	1	2	3	4	T
TCU	24	7	21	14	66
NM	7	10	0	0	17

The Frogs pose with the Mountain West championship trophy in the locker room following TCU's win over New Mexico.
Courtesy of Vladimir Cherry

MOUNTAIN WEST
FOOTBALL
REGULAR SEASON CHAMPIONS
2010
AIR FORCE
BYU
COLORADO STATE
NEW MEXICO
SAN DIEGO STATE
TCU
UNLV
UTAH
WYOMING

HORNED FROGS
62
61
76

Jeremy Kerley, left, and Josh Boyce celebrate after one of Boyce's two first-quarter touchdowns against Utah in Salt Lake City. *AP Images*

Jake Kirkpatrick (left) bumps fists with Andy Dalton after TCU's 45-0 home win over Wyoming on Oct. 9, 2010. *Richard W. Rodriguez, Special to the Star-Telegram*